Dear Anita

I hope

these wa... ent

Deeda encouraging

and inspirational

TO:

Anita

Love from

Anne

BUDDHISM FOR YOU

Courage

BUDDHISM FOR YOU

Courage

DAISAKU IKEDA

MIDDLEWAY
PRESS

Published by Middleway Press
A division of the SGI-USA
606 Wilshire Blvd., Santa Monica, CA 90401

© 2006 Soka Gakkai

Design by Lightbourne, Inc.

10 9 8 7 6 5 4 3 2

Library of Congress Cataloging-in-Publication Data

Ikeda, Daisaku.
    Buddhism for you. Courage / Daisaku Ikeda.
        p. cm.

    ISBN-13: 978-0-9723267-6-6 (hardcover : alk. paper)
    1. Religious life--Soka Gakkai. 2. Courage--Religious aspects--
Buddhism. I. Title.
BQ8499.I384B833 2006
294.3'5696--dc22

                                2006028526

ISBN: 978-0-9723267-6-6

Courage is the absolute condition
for becoming happy.

✳

There has never been, nor will there ever be, a
Buddha who does not encounter hardships.
Only by struggling against difficulties can
we attain the life-state of Buddhahood.
Herein lies the essence of Buddhism.

✳

To discard the shallow and seek the profound
is the way of a person of courage.

—*Nichiren*

Cheerfulness is not the same as frivolity.
Cheerfulness is born of a fighting spirit.
Frivolity is one manifestation
of cowardly escape.

❋

Courage is more exhilarating than fear.

—*Eleanor Roosevelt*

❋

War and oppression are not acts of
courage but of cowardice.

Great individuals fight abuses of authority.

✳

Those who have *no* courage are the ones
who steal, who oppress, who kill and maim,
who threaten people with weapons, who wage war.
People do such evil things because they are cowards.

✳

Let us give something to each person we meet:
joy, courage, hope, assurance, philosophy,
wisdom, a vision for the future.
Let us always give something.

*S*mall things matter.
What may look like a small act of courage
is courage nevertheless. The important thing
is to be willing to take a step forward.

✳

*T*rue courage is always backed by compassion;
there is nothing evil or malicious behind it.
If there is any ill intention, you can be sure
it is not real courage.

The essence of Buddhism is compassion. We, too, need to have compassion but, being ordinary mortals, the reality is that it is quite difficult for us. Courage substitutes for compassion. I am speaking of the courage to save others from suffering, to improve ourselves, to do our human revolution. To practice Buddhism with courage translates into compassion.

—*Josei Toda*

True courage means carrying out just and
beneficial activities; it means living honestly.
This is the most priceless sort of courage.

❄

Those who lack courage stray from
the correct path and succumb to apathy,
negativity and destructive ways.

❄

Those who are strong when
they stand alone possess true courage.

—*Friedrich von Schiller*

Courage comes from the wish
to do what's right, to build a just society
and to be a good human being.

Martin Luther King Jr. declared,
"Evil is ultimately doomed by the
powerful, inexorable forces of good."
Good means standing on the side of the people,
standing on the side of respect for life.

You should not have the
slightest fear in your heart.
It is lack of courage that prevents
one from attaining Buddhahood.

—*Nichiren*

9

It is not easy for people to exhibit compassion.
Many people who claim to have compassion
are actually hypocrites. That is why courage
is a more apt word than compassion.
To courageously speak about what is right
is tantamount to compassion.
Courage and compassion are like
two sides of the same coin.

✳

Bravely overcoming one small fear gives you
the courage to take on the next step.

Courageous action on the part of the young
is the source from which all else is created.
And it is conviction that guides and
lends support to courage.

✳

Only when people have the
courage to stand up for justice,
even if they are the only one,
can they lead the world in
the direction of peace and good.

✳

Always do what you are afraid to do.
—*Ralph Waldo Emerson*

Happiness as well as the real proof
of being alive lies in the will to
challenge yourself continuously,
unbroken and undefeated by anything.
Hold fast to courageous faith, always striving
to the very end in every field of endeavor.

✳

Our greatest ideas or plans, our
boundless compassion for others—all of
these will come to nothing unless we have
the courage to put them into action.
Without action, it's as if they never existed.

We should not dwell on the past;
there is no need to do so.
Those who exert themselves fully in the
present moment and burn with great hope
for the future are the true sages in life.

❋

Buddhahood is the greatest courage
and strongest life force there is.

❋

To live a victorious life requires the courage
to speak out for justice and the will to
show others the way to true freedom.

No matter what anyone else may say,
always do what you believe is right.
If you have the courage to do that, it's like
having a magical weapon of unlimited powers.
In Buddhism, we call such a person a bodhisattva,
one dedicated to relieving the suffering of others.

✳

When praised highly by others, one feels that
there is no hardship one cannot bear. Such is the
courage that springs from words of praise.

—*Nichiren*

If we are to do good, not only for ourselves
but for humanity and the world as well,
we need courage.

✳

Courage is the price that life extracts
for granting peace.
—*Amelia Earhart*

✳

A mother's feeling for her
children is a perfect example of
courage and compassion.

The courageous person wins.

The human will is an asset equally distributed among everyone, and any individual can allow it to manifest itself from one's inner possible resources if one has a mind to do so.

We must never give up our commitment to peace, our desire to learn and our love for humanity.
Putting those ideals into practice and spreading them among others is an act of courage.

Rather than lift your voice in a
thousand laments at the encroaching darkness,
light a single candle!

✳

Each of you should summon up the
courage of a lion king and never succumb
to threats from anyone.
The lion king fears no other beast,
nor do its cubs.

—*Nichiren*

Courage is the invincible jeweled sword
that cuts through all adversity.

❋

Confront reality, look it squarely in the face,
and with guts, wisdom and strength,
challenge everything that lies ahead of you.

Strengthen your faith day by day and month after month. Should you slacken in your resolve even a bit, devils will take advantage.

—*Nichiren*

Courageous people are first masters of their own heart.

No matter how wonderful our dreams, how noble our ideals, or how high our hopes, ultimately we need courage to make them a reality in the face of sufferings and hurdles.

✳

Continue forging ahead despite any storms or hardships that may arise. Be fearless and advance like a lion.

One who has mastered himself is truly free.
Freedom lies in the heart of the sage,
servitude in the heart of the fool.

Hope is courage.

✳

The secret to victory in any struggle
is fervent prayer. The next step is
boldly to take action.
Maintaining courage, hope and perseverance,
let us inspire everyone to action and encourage
each other toward victory. This is the formula
for winning in any endeavor.

The truly strong do not
lord it over the weak.

✳

The Buddha wrote that one should become
the master of one's mind rather than
let one's mind master oneself.

—*Nichiren*

Struggling against great difficulty
enables us to develop ourselves tremendously.
Difficulties can be a source of dynamic
new growth and positive progress.

✳

Sincere words of encouragement
have the power to give people hope
and courage to go on living.

At a crucial moment it is the strength and courage of ordinary people who have no name or position in society that save the day.

＊

Courage is free. Anyone can have it.

＊

When we encounter prejudice, we need to challenge and destroy it without hesitation, on the spot.

The life of a person who shrinks before oppression and tries to get by with cunning strategies and falsehood is extremely pitiful. Such a life is self-defeating.

Rather, by fighting against and pushing through all the evil that oppresses one, both internally and externally, one establishes a magnanimous self and a profound and happy state of life. This is the purpose of faith.

Though evils may be numerous, they cannot prevail over a single great truth, just as many raging fires are quenched by a single shower of rain. This principle also holds true with Nichiren and his followers.

—*Nichiren*

Courageous people can overcome anything.

Without courage there is no happiness
and it is impossible to create a life of value.
This is an unchanging rule of human existence.

✳

The deeper the darkness, the more crucial it is
for us to make our lives shine like the sun and
brilliantly illuminate the surrounding gloom.
This is the way of Buddhism.

Joy is found in struggle . . . it is found
in the darkness of the crushing breakers
and tearing winds of a stormy sea.

—*Alexander Pushkin*

✳

Bodhisattvas are courageous individuals
who plunge headlong into the thick of society
to lead others to happiness.

Faced with what is right, to leave it undone
shows a lack of courage.

—*Confucius*

People of true courage always stand alone.

There is no need to hold back in the struggle against injustice. We should speak the truth plainly, exposing evil for what it is.

❋

Those who stand up at a crucial moment demonstrate genuine greatness. They are people who leave an immortal history.

Courage is one of the most
important things in life.
Courage also lies at the core of the
writings of Nichiren, who declares,
"Nichiren's disciples cannot accomplish
anything if they are cowardly."

As the inner state of Buddhahood is strengthened,
we also develop a fortitude that enables us to
ride even the wildest storms. If we are
enlightened to the true, unchanging
nature of life, we can joyfully surf the
waves of difficulty that wash against us in life,
creating something of value out of any situation.
In this way our "true self" blossoms, and we find vast
reserves of courage, compassion, wisdom and energy
or life force inside us. We find ourselves becoming
more active and feeling deep inner freedom.

You cannot discover and realize your
purpose in life with halfhearted efforts.
To follow the dream in your heart and
fulfill your mission requires true courage.

✳

Buddhism exists in society,
not in temples or hermitages.
The true Buddhist spirit is to take
courageous action for the betterment of society.

Inazo Nitobe, the respected Japanese
educator and diplomat said,
"Faith is courage as courage is faith.
Cheerfulness marks a great soul . . .
In the heat of battles which would fret the
mediocre, a great soul keeps up cheer."

✳

To be fearless no matter what happens—
that is the root of true happiness.

The cause of peace will be advanced by brave people armed with the spirit of independence who voluntarily strive to fulfill the vow they made. Because they struggle on their own volition, they have no complaints or grievances.

❋

Great good entails combating great evil. Courageously walk the path of great good throughout your lives.

The courage to fight for truth and justice embodies great good, and those who possess such courage are praiseworthy above all.

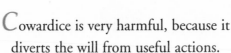

Cowardice is very harmful, because it diverts the will from useful actions.

—*René Descartes*

Life is best lived by being bold and daring.
People tend to grow fearful when they taste failure,
face a daunting challenge or fall ill. Yet that is
precisely the time to become even bolder.
Those who are victors at heart
are the greatest of all champions.

❋

The most important kind of courage is the
courage required to live a good life each day.

To move forward resolutely regardless of what lies in store—that is the spirit, the resolve, that leads to human victory.

✳

Fear is hell; courage is joy.

✳

The courage to continue to speak out for what is right and just is certain to shake people's preconceived notions, cause them to question their beliefs and awaken their hearts and minds.

42

Nonviolence is not a cover for cowardice,
but it is the supreme virtue of the brave.

—*Mahatma Gandhi*

If we allow ourselves to be disturbed by
petty criticism and slander, if we fear
pressure or persecution, we will
never create anything
of lasting value.

To hope to attain Buddhahood
without speaking out against slander
is as futile as trying to find water in the
midst of fire or fire in the midst of water.

—*Nichiren*

To transform your life into
a happy one, you need courage.
Genuine happiness is found in courage.
Courage is the gateway to happiness.

❋

Rosa Parks, the mother of
the civil rights movement, found the courage
to speak out because she believed she was right.
Courage always springs from
what is right, from justice.

The person who has the courage
to say what needs to be said,
no matter what the circumstances, and
to take action when action is called for
will definitely attain Buddhahood.

The German poet Johann Wolfgang von Goethe declared that the loss of possessions and reputation is insignificant because you can always set out to restore them, whereas the loss of courage is the loss of everything.

❄

Courageous young people are always catalysts for reform. It is vital that youth become strong and initiate change from the grassroots level, from the bottom up.

We can never hope to win if we
have a wavering, indecisive attitude.
We mustn't be cowardly.
Only the courageous can win
over themselves and triumph in life.

❋

Faith is not emotionalism. Faith is courage.
To become happy, we must have courage.

Meeting new people and
opening fresh channels of communication
require courage and initiative.

On the flip side of arrogance lies cowardice—
a lack of courage to face the truth.
Likewise, discrimination and envy are
also two sides of the same coin.

"Of all base passions, fear is most accursed."
This declaration, from Shakespeare,
calls on us to lead lives of courage
and to act intrepidly for justice and
people's happiness; it implies that cowards,
because they are ruled by fear, are pitiful.

Courage always stirs a response.

53

If you give serious thought to the happiness of your friends and the welfare of your society and community—racking your brains over how you can contribute, taking action to try to make a difference—then you will find vibrant wisdom welling forth from your life. Courage will rise within you quite naturally.

We must win in life.
Even if we suffer minor defeats and
setbacks along the way, it is important
that we triumph in the end, that we strive
toward ultimate victory with unceasing effort
and courage, with the ardent resolve to
definitely win. If we win, we will gain
a great sense of fulfillment and joy.

Hope is born of the courage and enthusiasm that does not shrink from real effort and hard work.

✳

One who has the courage to speak the truth lives a truly splendid and fulfilling life.

Those who can't do anything but live cowardly lives
are like beasts. They are ignoble and unhappy.
Those who live out their lives courageously,
on the other hand, lead the noblest and
most sublime existences;
they are happy.

—*Josei Toda*

❋

Without courage we cannot be compassionate.

*Additional books in this series
are available and include:*

Determination
Love
Prayer

To order please visit:
www.MiddlewayPress.com

*For more information about the SGI,
please visit:* www.sgi-usa.org